ADULT
Conversations

ROBERT COLLINS

Copyright © 2022 Robert Collins.

All rights reserved. No part of this book may be reproduced, stored, or transmitted by any means—whether auditory, graphic, mechanical, or electronic—without written permission of both publisher and author, except in the case of brief excerpts used in critical articles and reviews. Unauthorized reproduction of any part of this work is illegal and is punishable by law.

ISBN: 979-8-88640-220-9 (sc)
ISBN: 979-8-88640-221-6 (hc)
ISBN: 979-8-88640-222-3 (e)

Because of the dynamic nature of the Internet, any web addresses or links contained in this book may have changed since publication and may no longer be valid. The views expressed in this work are solely those of the author and do not necessarily reflect the views of the publisher, and the publisher hereby disclaims any responsibility for them.

One Galleria Blvd., Suite 1900, Metairie, LA 70001
1-888-421-2397

ENDORSEMENTS

"Adult Conversations is a great reference book. The tool described in Collins' interesting vignettes evokes familiar instances and examples that can be helpful when stuck for a communications solution."

Dr. Milli Pierce, Author and Educator

"Robert uses everyday life experiences to adroitly demonstrate the need for and use of his tool for effective communication. The tool is simple but effective. Think how much the world would benefit if the world community could stop to master these simple techniques."

Rudolph Pierce former Justice of the Massachusetts Superior Court

"This work of non-fiction is an excellent tool for those who seek a better means of positive and constructive communication. While the lessons are shared by way of short stories, their messages are universal regardless of race, religion, age or cultural heritage."

Francis E. Jackson, Jr. Attorney at Law

AMAZON REVIEWS

Kindle Customer
5.0 out of 5 stars
Good Communication
Reviewed in the United States on November 25, 2019
This book is an useful tool in the communication process. The author define the different egos we have in layman terms. It's a precise and with great clarity. You will see yourself in many of the examples. Wow! Quick Goodread

Tai Hunte
5.0 out of 5 stars
What a wonderful way to explain such an important concept
Reviewed in the United States on September 24, 2014
What a wonderful way to explain such an important concept. This book is an excellent read that brings the reader to the most healthy method of communication. The stories give an amazing and unique approach to share wisdom surrounding an extremely common deficiency among humans. I loved all of the stories that highlighted points in various situations. Any reader can identify with at least one story. I found the one I identified personally with and am definitely on my way to improving my communication skills. It was an easy and fun read that I think everyone can learn from!

Elizabeth A. Powell
5.0 out of 5 stars
This is a great book. It is appropriate for anyone in a ...
Reviewed in the United States on September 27, 2014
This is a great book. It is appropriate for anyone in a relationship, or who has been in one! Communication is the key to a lasting relationship with spouses, partners, family members, co workers....learn how to make the best of your interactions. The book was easy to read, has lots of personal vignettes, and is a good handbook to keep nearby to refer to again and again. The author's communication tool is so logical, there's no way it wouldn't work!

M A Washington
5.0 out of 5 stars
Funny and Informative
Reviewed in the United States on October 7, 2014
I enjoyed reading this book not only because my brother wrote it, which in itself is a good reason, but also I learned something about how people interact...PAC. ALTHOUGH SOME NAMES WERE CHANGED IT WAS INTERESTING LOOKING INTO HIS HISTORY AND READING ABOUT STORIES IN HIS PAST. For those in a relationship or that about to get in one a good tool in how to communicate.

Frances M. Benjamin
4.0 out of 5 stars
Lessons for all
Reviewed in the United States on December 1, 2014
I enjoyed the wisdom of this book and the way the author used personal stories to teach the PAC lessons. A short but enjoyable read that anyone can apply to their own interactions and relationships with children, partners, friends, or even strangers.

Damiana Gonzalez
5.0 out of 5 stars
Adult Conversations is one of the best books that I've ever read
Reviewed in the United States on October 24, 2014
Adult Conversations is one of the best books that I've ever read. It gives you the tools (PAC), you need to communicate more effectively. It's written to be easy to understand and incredibly practical. Although it's a short read that you could easily finish in a single afternoon, it's packed with profound wisdom. Give it a read, I have already used principles from the book and I can see a difference in my conversations. I can't recommend this book enough.

Dennis Dottin
5.0 out of 5 stars
MR COLLINS HAS TO BE A GREAT
Reviewed in the United States on December 17, 2014
A VERY INFORMATIVE INSIGHT ON A VERY IMPORTANT CONCEPT, MR COLLINS HAS TO BE A GREAT PARENT/HUSBAND

To Jesus Christ, my Lord and Savior.
To Him I give all the glory.

CONTENTS

Preface 1
Protocol 5
Prelude 6
Annette's Adult 7
David and Goliath 8
Do Not Provoke The Parent 9
Peace 10
Think 11
Do Not Abuse Alcohol or Drugs 12
Wisdom 13
Ask and It Shall be Given 15
You Cannot Park Here 17
Yelling and Screaming at Each Other 18
Play by the Same Rules 19
Tactical Approach to Communication 20
Bus Ride 21
Jesus' Child 23
Shutting Down the Federal Government 24
Twenty-Nine Years of Marriage 25
Gubernatorial Candidate 26
Chess Extraordinaire 27
Like Mother like Child 29
Chess Tournament 30
Don't Sit on the Banister 31
Do You Know How to Change a Tire? 32
Shopping with the Wife 33
Guilty 35
Pastor's Parent 37

Here Comes the Devil	39
Conversation with God	41
Here Comes the Judge	42
Judge	43
My Father-in-Law	44
My Mother-in-Law	46
Honor Your Father and Mother and You Shall Have Long Life	47
Whatever You Do to the Least of Them, You Have Done unto Me!	49
As a Man Thinks—So is He	50
Blocking Traffic	51
Making Love	52
Mom, Are You Upset about Something?	53
Foursome	55
Peter	56
Don't Let the Sun Go down on Your Anger	57
Don't Let Anyone Else Drive My Car	58
My Brother-in-Law	59
Passing It On	60
Riding to Work	61
Worse, It's Milli!	62
Haircut	63
How Not to Treat a Lady	65
The Hairpiece	66
Bullfoot	67
Raise	69
Single Mother	70
Frustration on the Job	72
Three Hundred and Sixty Degrees	74
It's all about Jesus and His Word	84
Conclusion	86
Acknowledgments	87
About the Author	88
About the book	89

PREFACE

Approximately forty years ago, I read a book entitled: *"What Do You Say After You Say Hello?* by Eric Berne, MD. This book changed my life, and I hope my book, *Adult Conversations*, will change countless other peoples' lives.

> Bible Translations Referenced:
> > The KJV Study Bible
> > New Living Translation
> > The Rainbow Study Bible

The concept of my book comes straight from *What Do You Say After You Say Hello?* I present actual situations that are not unique to me and demonstrate how I would apply the principals in his book to solve the communication problems.

To begin, let me describe how the concept in Dr. Berne's book applies:

> *My people are destroyed for lack of knowledge: (Hosea 6:3)*

* * *

Why Parent, Adult, and Child, because of its Simplicity.

Saying Parent, Adult, or Child conjures up images familiar to all of us. If I were to say Superego, Alter ego, or Mild ego, these words may mean different or unclear things to each of us.

The Parent represents directives, commands, orders, instructions, and so forth. For example:

> *"Do this or don't do that."*
> *"Get up or go to bed."*
> *"I told you so."*
> *"Why don't you listen?"*
> *"Be careful."*
> *"Do you want me to beat you?"*
> *"I said shut up!"*

and so forth and so on.

When we speak like this or hear someone talking about these things, we know immediately they are in the Parent ego state. The point is not that the Parent is a bad thing. It just gives us clarity as to where the communication is coming from.

There's nothing wrong with having a strong Parent. Sometimes it is necessary. My point is just to make you aware of this state of mind that we all have.

Even children display a Parent when they are playing. One will talk like the Parent:

> *"I said do this or do that."*
> *"you better listen to me or else."*

An example of the Parent: A wife comes home and sees her husband's clothes all over the place.

"Why don't you put your clothes where they belong?" she asks. *"I don't think I should have to pick up your mess. You're a grown man, why don't you act like one?"*

Everyone has three ego states: Parent, Adult, and Child. You are always in one of these ego states at any given time. It is important to remember that this is just a tool to tell what frame of mind someone is in and why.

For example: A police officer will have a strong Parent ego state, because, when he speaks, he is usually giving orders or commands and expects to be obeyed. He says:

> *"Stop!"*
> *"Keep moving!"*
> *"Let me see your hands."*

And so forth and so on.

> Teachers have strong Parent ego states:
> *"Be quiet."*
> *"No talking."*
> *"Open your books."*
> *"What is the answer?"*

By now, I am hoping you are getting the picture of what makes up the Parent.

The Child consists of your emotions: laughing, crying, passions, sentiments, excitements, sensations, reactions, feelings, envy, screaming, sadness, and happiness. When you hear a funny joke, you laugh. That is the Child. When you hurt and are miserable, you're in your Child ego state. When you're scared and can't function, that is the Child. When you're furious because somebody did something wrong to you, that is the Child. In short, the Child is simply a way of saying that your emotions are in control.

An example of the Child: A mother or father may tell children to go to bed, and they start to protest: "We don't want to go to bed now.

> They may even start crying:
> **"Please don't make me go to bed."**
> **"I want to stay up for a little while longer."**

The mother or father might say,
*"I don't care what you want.
Just do as you're told and go to bed."*

As you can imagine, this conversation between the Parent and Child can go on indefinitely.

A comedian's lifeblood depends on him hooking the Child in his audience. The emotional part of his audience's character.

Both the Parent and the Child are recordings made from the time you were born to about the age of seven. The recordings come from observations of all the people around you.

We see this when children are playing: one will be the Parent, telling the other kids what to do, and the kids, acting like children, will obey.

The Adult is what we develop on our own, usually from reading and experiences. You may have also overheard information that developed the Adult or someone may have spoken to your spirit. You can also observe something that will develop the Adult.

The Adult is the problem-solving, rational thinker. He listens and questions things with an open mind. He also responds to ideas and concepts in a way that leaves no question about who is in charge. An example of the Adult: *"Robert, I want you to write a book."*

The Parent: *"I will not write a book. I don't know how."*

The Child: *"Tell me to do anything, but don't ask me to write a book. I don't have the ability or discipline to write a book."*

The Adult: *"Wow! Write a book? I am not sure if I can, but I am willing to try."*

PROTOCOL

A very important point to keep in mind as you read my stories is the way these egos interact with each other. The Parent and Child can communicate endlessly. The Parent can communicate with another Parent or Child and the Child can communicate with another Child or Parent. But, and this is a big BUT, the Adult can only communicate with another Adult. Never can the Adult communicate with the Parent or Child.

To understand how simply this tool works, you must understand the protocol.

Example of how this works

You may ask your spouse (Adult):
"Do you know where my car keys are?"

They may answer in the Parent and say:
"If you put them where they belong, you would know where they are." *(Instruction-belongs to the Parent)*

He or she may also answer in the Child and say:
"I didn't touch them, so don't blame me if they are lost."
(Sensitive –part of the Child.)

They could also answer in the Adult and say:
"No I don't know where your keys are, but I will help you look for them."

PRELUDE

Have you ever been in the middle of a conversation and realized you have no clue how it escalated into an argument? Sure you have. We all have. This is the point of an Adult Conversation. When you find yourself in a place other than in the Adult, this book will give you the tool to navigate your way back to a safe haven. It does this by giving you a collection of stories that demonstrate how to use this tool in each situation.

As we begin on this journey of communications, may God Bless those who have ears to hear.

ANNETTE'S ADULT

Even children can have a strong Adult.

My five year old daughter Annette and I were sitting in my car outside her grammar school. A man who was selling children's books walked up to us and wanted to know if I would buy one. I said, "I didn't want to buy any." He said they were great books and my daughter would love them. He was very persistent. Finally, hoping this would persuade him to leave, I said I don't have any money. He continued, "Well, if you don't have any money, I will trade my books for your car."

I gave a little laugh and started to drive away. Then my daughter asked why I didn't trade with him. I replied by asking her if she really thought that was a good deal to trade my car for some books. She said, "Sure, books will take you anywhere you want to go."

I was astonished at the wisdom of her thinking. That was the Adult in her speaking.

DAVID AND GOLIATH

My children, Robert Jr and Annette were playing (Child) and chasing each other around the house. Robert was fourteen and about six feet tall. Annette was ten years old and only four feet ten. When I looked, I saw Annette had Robert trapped in the kitchen corner ready to pounce on him. I said, "Annette, aren't you afraid of him? He is so big."

She said, "no, David wasn't afraid of Goliath!"

Again, this was the Adult in her speaking, based on her knowledge and reasoning of the Bible.

DO NOT PROVOKE THE PARENT

My Daughter snatched the remote out of my hand (Child) while I was watching an important show. She changed the channel and then refused to give it back.

I chased (hooking my Child) her around the house, trying to get the remote so I would not miss the conclusion. I was getting very angry (Child) because I could not get her to understand how much I wanted to see the end of the program. I was so angry, that if I had gotten my hands on her, I would have given her a good spanking. That is when I caught myself and gave up the chase.

I sat down on the couch and didn't speak until I cooled off. When she realized the chase was over, Annette gave me back the remote. I told her (Adult), "Not now, but tomorrow we need to talk.

She sensed something happened between us, and it went far beyond the moment. We made a date for lunch the following day and I told her about the Parent, Adult, and Child ego states. I explained what happened yesterday should not have happened but more importantly, it should never happen again." Once we had a basic understanding of how to communicate with each other, we assured ourselves that it will never happen again.

Annette hooked my Child by snatching the remote. I was very upset and didn't like how I was feeling, communication stopped. Since the adult cannot communicate with the child, I sat down on the couch and calmly told her the next day we were going to meet for lunch and talk about what took place that day.

PEACE

I was at peace, sitting in my living room, when my wife came in yelling and screaming at me about the messy back yard.

"You don't (Parent) cut the grass, pick up the trash, or take proper care of the surroundings anymore. You ought to be ashamed of yourself!"

She continued on in that fashion for about two or three minutes. When I didn't open my mouth to utter one word, she stormed out of the room as angrily as she had stormed in. Ten minutes later, she came back to the room, where I was still recovering from the shock of her prior visit, to apologize. She knew about (PAC), the Parent, Adult, Child and when she didn't hook my Child, she had no choice, but to leave, because there was no communication. Parent cannot communicate with the Adult. So, she came back to reestablish communication Adult to Adult. At that point, we were able to work things out and still respect each other.

We both ended up getting what we wanted: She got a clean yard and I was able to remain at peace.

THINK

Thinking, it may sound easy, but not always possible, when you're in the heat of battle. The day my wife came into the living room and started to berate me about cleaning the yard, I had a choice: I could have responded in my Parent and said, "Who are you to tell me what to do?" I could even have reacted in my Child, gotten furious, and started yelling back at her. Instead, I thought for several minutes and decided the best course of action was to not speak at all. (Adult).

The tool [PAC] is so embedded in my mind that I instinctively responded correctly by keeping my mouth shut. My hope and purpose of this book is that this concept will become second nature to all who want an alternative way to communicate.

DO NOT ABUSE ALCOHOL OR DRUGS

The reason I do not drink anymore or do drugs is because when you're under the influence, you are automatically in your Child. Remember, feelings and emotions are all part of your Child. Your ability to reason as an Adult is greatly impaired. When you're having a few drinks or drunk you feel happy, mad, or you may become depressed. In short, your emotions are in control.

Some people abuse their spouses or children, using the excuse that they were drunk and didn't know what they were doing. Some people have trouble communicating when they are sober, so just imagine what happens when they get drunk they act like a fool and God doesn't like fools.

Personally, I want to stay in my Adult, as much as possible. From my own history, I know for a fact, this is impossible once you take something to alter your mind such as drugs or alcohol.

WISDOM

*And God gave Solomon wisdom and exceedingly
great understanding, and largeness of heart
like the sand on the seashore
(1 Kings 4:29).*

King Solomon could have asked God for anything, but he asked for wisdom. Wisdom and the Adult are like wet to water: If you are using Wisdom you are probably operating in your Adult. They both come primarily from reading and experiences. We get knowledge in four ways:

Reading
Listening and/or Overhearing
Observing and/or Watching.
Experiences

Reading is the best. When we read, our minds are updating or recording constantly like a computer.

I let my feelings of lust (Child) rule my judgment and as a result another woman later became pregnant. Although it turned out to be a lie, it ruined my marriage. After ten years of being single, I decided to marry again, but made a vow to myself to never cheat on my wife again.—Adult-Wisdom. In recognition of what happened before I had learned from my mistakes.

Six months after I was married, the first test came. I was away at training in Atlanta, Georgia when I met a woman who took me to a hotel. Before I knew what was happening we were both naked and ready for a sexual encounter. My Adult kicked in, and I said, "Stop!"

The Child said, "Are you crazy? Not now." However, the wisdom of my Adult ruled the day and no sexual escapade happened. I kept my vow and thirty-eight (38) years later, I continue honoring this vow and my wonderful marriage

ASK AND IT SHALL BE GIVEN

Walking through K-Mart, I saw a lady sitting down with what appeared to be a world of concern on her face. "What happened? Are you okay?" I asked. She said, "Yes," it's just that I don't know how to talk to my mother, and it frustrates me. She is elderly and everything I say to her ends up in a fight." Sara talks to her mother in her Parent:

"Ma, go to the front of the store and pay for your goods"
- (Parent commands-directives)

Her mother responds in her Adult:

*"I am waiting for you so we can leave together.
When I am finished, I won't have to come
all the way back here to get you."*

Sara's Child comes out and she gets angry.

*"Just go and come back here when you finish. I am
exasperated and worn out and don't want to walk anymore.
I have been walking all day, so just do as I say and when
you come back, we will leave by the side door."*

I asked Sara if she has problems communicating with only her mother, and she said "No!" apparently, she has trouble communicating with her husband all the time, and she doesn't know what to do. When he does not respond as she expects, she just clams up and ends communication for fear it may escalate into an argument.

I suggested my concept to her and explained about her having a very strong Parent and Child and to my surprise she agreed. She likes to tell everyone what to do and think and she closes up and gets angry when people don't listen.

In the scenario with her mother, the mother has a strong Adult and the daughter has a strong Parent. The mother wants to reason and use logic, whereas the daughter wants to command and direct.

With her husband, it sounds like the same thing, except he also has a strong Child. So, when she commands, his response is anger.

This is the classic model of the Parent to Child. The Parent and Child can communicate continually but neither one can communicate with the Adult.

YOU CANNOT PARK HERE

At 7:30 p.m., it was dark, crowded and men were drinking and smoking as I pulled up to park at my warehouse. I store my electronic parts that I use on my job as a technician, in my warehouse which happens to be across the street from a nightclub. I was greeted by "you can't park here!" Which was clearly his Parent- command.

"Hey, he said you can't park here."

My choice was to park anyway and to not answer him. If I answered, I would have had to go into my Parent: by saying "Don't tell me where I can park." Or my Child: "How come I can't park here?"

I got out of my car while he kept saying I couldn't do what I was doing. Ignoring the person, I took out my warehouse keys so I could unload my parts. When he saw what I was doing, he didn't say another word. He realized I had the right to park where I did in order to take care of my business. If I tried to explain this to him beforehand, it could easily have led to an argument: This may have resulted in a Child-to-Child conversation but I easily avoided this by choosing to stay in my Adult and not respond.

Again because I recognized immediately that the guy was in his Child or Parent, I was able to defuse the situation by just ignoring him and going about my business. He quickly realized that I had a perfect right to park and proceed with my business.

I was able to hook his Adult by not saying a word.

YELLING AND SCREAMING AT EACH OTHER

At 6:30 a.m. a son was getting ready to go to work. His father and mother went down to see him off, when his mother noticed he was high from smoking marijuana. She started questioning him about going to work high. He started to yell that he knew what he was doing, saying everyone told him it was okay to smoke as long as he worked hard. This answer immediately hooked his father's Child because it sounded so ridiculous.

The father started yelling, asking his son for names of the people who told him this. The son gave his father names, trying to justify his statement, but the yelling continued. They were all communicating Child to Child.

The mother was yelling, telling the son that he wreaked of marijuana and suggested that he was crazy to believe no one would notice. Since all parties involved are communicating by yelling this encounter could last for hours. {Child to Child} The mother was now crying, as the son was still yelling that he knows what he was doing. The father was yelling, "Sure, just like when you played ball in high school, thinking you could play better while high. Or when you went to college and got kicked out because you were getting high."

Finally, the father walked away because he chose to not communicate in his Child any longer. Once the son got high, he was automatically in his Child because being high allowed his emotions to take control. He became lethargic, emotional lazy and his thinking was altered.

The son left the home mad and the mother remained emotionally shaken long after the argument had ended. The father approached his wife in his Parent (remember the Parent and Child go hand-in-hand) and said, "Let's put him out of the house. This will be the only way he will learn."

She said, "No."

The Adult never showed up in this conversation. I believe it never had a chance to.

PLAY BY THE SAME RULES

If baseball players all used different rules while playing the game, there would be chaos on the field. The same rule of thumb is applicable to all games. Chess, golf, poker—everything.

This is the premise of using this tool when it comes to communication: Parent, Adult, and Child.

The concept of parent, adult and child ego states influencing communication is effective when everyone plays by the same rules.

TACTICAL APPROACH TO COMMUNICATION

*Wife: "Why do you have to close the bathroom window at night?
(A new air-conditioner was installed the previous month.)*

*Husband: "I close the window so the unit can
be more efficient. Why do you ask?"*

*Wife: "You don't open it in the morning. It makes
the bathroom smell and creates mildew."*

*Husband: "Okay, either I won't close the window
or I will open it in the morning."*

Conclusion: this is an Adult ego state styled conversation.

BUS RIDE

A bus picked up several of us for an excursion of the country of the Dominican Republic—a two-and-a-half-hour trip to tour the city of Santo Domingo.

I sat up front with my wife and we had a great view of the countryside. The rest of the family sat right behind us. It was a wonderful ride with several stops along the way.

After six hours in the city, it was time to head back to the resort where we were staying at called Punta Cana. Initially, when we got back on the bus, I saw that another couple had taken our seats.

Adult: "Hey, this is our seat, so please get up and give it back to us."
Child: *The couple completely ignored me.*

This hooked my Child, and I appealed to the excursion leader.

"This couple took our seats. Can you please tell them to move?"

His reply was, "I can't really tell them anything. The seats are not assigned to anyone."

I continued, "we rode here the whole way in these seats and our stuff is in the bin above the seat."

Again, the excursion leader stated, "I hear you and I'm sorry, but there is nothing I can do."

Now I was angry as hell. Then enters my wicked Child who is coming out and wants to grab the man and force him to get out of our seats. My wife appealed to my Adult and said, "let it go and we will move to others seats.

Trying to use better judgment, I decided to listen to her and we moved, Needless to say, I was not happy (Child). While sitting in the back of the bus, I was plotting how to get even with him: There were thoughts of throwing a bottle of water on him, curse him, or just wait until we made another scheduled stop reclaim possession of my seat.

Clearly, my Child was in control the entire time and I couldn't relax or enjoy the return trip.

One hour and a half later, my opportunity came when the bus stopped and the couple got off the bus. I took my seat (Child) and was still furious, hoping they would say something to me when they came back on the bus. I had a horrible and mean reply ready for them, but they didn't say a word when they came back on the bus.

This is a classic case of staying in my Child, although I knew better. I wanted my pound of their flesh and refused to talk myself out of extracting it. If the man in particular had only given me a reason why they wanted that seat, I could have worked with him, but he completely ignored me and that brought out the worst (my wicked Child) in me.

JESUS' CHILD

When Jesus walked into the synagogue and saw that the Jews had turned it into a place to gamble and bargain he got angry. He said they had turned his Father's house into a den of thieves.

This hooked his Child (emotions) and he got angry. He started turning over tables and chairs. His disciples tried to stop him, but he was out of control and continued to turn over all the tables.

Conclusion: everybody, including the Son of God, has the three ego states. When he was teaching, he was in his Parent: giving instructions, demonstrations, and miracles. His Adult: when his disciples asked him to show them the Father, his Adult response was, "If you have known me ye should have known the Father also. John 8:19

> *"I have placed before you life and death; choose life."*
> *(Deut. 30:19)*

These are just a few examples of his Adult conversations.

SHUTTING DOWN THE FEDERAL GOVERNMENT

10/13/2013

This is a classic case of Parent-to-Child communication.

President Barack Obama said, "Obama Care is the law. This point is non-negotiable" (Parent).

Republican Speaker of the House John Boehner responded: "Oh Yeah?" (Child).

The Affordable Care Act also known as Obamacare, is the law and both political parties needed to recognize this fact.

Adult: "Let's find common ground and move forward."

TWENTY-NINE YEARS OF MARRIAGE

I get along pretty well with my wife. We both understand how this communication concept works. We apply this tool when necessary. Without this tool, I am not sure, we would be as happy as we are. I can detect where my wife is coming from and gauge the correct response. We still have our differences, but we also have no problem instituting the solution.

Case in point: yesterday when I walked into the house, the TV was on the Spanish news channel. I told (Parent) my wife that I was changing the channel to English-speaking news broadcast. That way, we could both listen to the news. I hooked her Child. She got angry.

"I was listening to that station to hear what they were going to say."

I didn't respond (Adult) because I thought it was only fair that we put it on a channel that we both understood. She went up to the master bedroom to watch the news in Spanish. Later, when I needed to go up to the master bedroom, I told her she could have her TV back and watch her channel downstairs while she was cooking. Because I had to take a shower, I suggested that we could switch TVs. She said, "no!", because she is now adamant about watching the TV upstairs, even though it would have been more convenient for her to cook and watch it at the same time. I asked her if she was being sensible. I made an attempt to hook her Adult, but she was not falling for it. She didn't care about sensibility now because she was upset that I had changed the channel. I let it go. I knew, at that point, there would be no more communication on the subject.

GUBERNATORIAL CANDIDATE

The Candidate had a Chief of Staff who was efficient and productive. She kept things moving toward the Candidate's goal of becoming governor.

The Candidate is a lawyer and former judge. The Candidate developed a strong Parent by the nature of his training. The Candidate had an employee who happened to be the Chief of Staff's daughter. This employee did something to upset the Candidate and he fired the employee.

The Chief of Staff approached the Candidate and asked if they could both sit down and discuss what happened. The Candidate's response was to terminate the Chief of Staff without giving her an opportunity to speak. Clearly, the Adult was not in control. It was the Candidate's way or the highway. That is something that the Parent or wicked Child do.

"I don't care about what you think and I don't want to talk about it."

The Adult response is to listen to all sides of a conversation and then make an appropriate reply based on what transpired.

CHESS EXTRAORDINAIRE

John is a chess extraordinaire. Unfortunately, he also has a very strong Parent and Child. This is partly from his profession as a teacher and a principal for many years.

Several years ago, another chess enthusiast hooked his Child, and, up to now, he has refused to let the Adult take back control.

As the story goes, he was part of a chess club in the Virgin Islands that travels to all the Chess Olympiad tournaments around the world. Suzie, who was the president of the chess club, made most of the decisions regarding the club. She did most of the work in terms of soliciting money for the organization and setting up tournaments.

One day, Suzie requested information from John about a separate and distinct chess organization that he had formed in St. Thomas. Suzie's motivation was simply to justify asking the Virgin Islands Olympic Committee and the local government for additional funds for the Virgin Islands Chess Federation. John responded by saying the chess club was his baby and Suzie had no right to ask for any information about what he was doing or how much money he collected. That's a Child response: in other words, this is my toy and you cannot play with it.

This exchange of communication created a huge rift between the two organizations. Suzie's response was to block any person from St. Thomas from further participation in Chess Olympiads. St. Thomians would no longer have the opportunity to travel to any of these wonderful countries to play chess. (That was a Child-to-Child scenario: "I am angry, so this is what I am going to do.")

The other person said, "Oh yeah? Well, I am angry too and this is what I am going to do back to you."

John then wrote a contemptuous letter to the Virgin Islands Olympic Committee, alleging Suzie's inappropriate actions. The aftermath of that letter resulted in the Olympic Committee withdrawing what little financial support it was giving to the Virgin Islands Chess Federation. Additionally, John and Suzie stopped talking to each other.

What a calamity of events.

Try as we might, we cannot get John to reconcile with Suzie. He refuses to come out of his Child (being angry). Where is your Adult? After all, a greater cause needs to be addressed. The cause is bringing back the opportunity for the chess players of St. Thomas to travel as Chess Olympians all over the world.

Be an Adult and let's move on.

The point of this book is to show how the tool of Parent, Adult and Child work to give the reader the options he needs to adapt to the situation. The case above is important because this person may not know how to come out of his anger [Child] to deal with the real issue of reconciling differences for the betterment of the whole chess community.

LIKE MOTHER LIKE CHILD

Having just finished dinner at a restaurant, the family was dividing the bill. The daughter, who used a credit card for her portion, asked her mother (Adult) if the tip was included. The mother responded (Parent), "Just pay the bill."

That response hooked the daughter's Child and she countered by saying, "Don't tell me to just pay the bill. I just want to make sure I don't over tip. When you use a credit card, sometimes you still have to add a tip."

The mother's Parent said, "I said just pay what I told you to pay." This went back and forth for several minutes, with both the mother and daughter communicating (Parent to Child). It ended with the mother not speaking to the daughter. The daughter, still trying to make her point, was relentless until she got her pound of flesh.

If her mother had responded in her (Adult) from the beginning and said, "Yes, the tip is already included," and left out the part about, "Just pay the bill," then they would have avoided all confusion.

CHESS TOURNAMENT

Matthew was hosting a chess tournament at his law office. We were using a conference room that had antique furniture. While I was pondering a move, I leaned back in the chair so only two legs were touching the floor. The next thing I knew, the chair collapsed.

Well, Matthew was discombobulated. His Parent said,

> *"What are you doing? You don't know how to sit in a chair? Why did you do that? You're supposed to sit in a chair properly."*

He continued to engage in a fit of rage, almost to the point of losing control. He just kept scolding me.

> I tried to respond in my Adult and said,
> *"I did not mean to break the chair."*

He was not to be assuaged. He was to the point of being out of control. I then said very forcefully, **"Look, get a grip on yourself. It was an unfortunate accident."**

Finally, I hooked his Adult and he realized there was nothing left to do but to let it go. At that point, we were able to continue the chess tournament.

DON'T SIT ON THE BANISTER

Rosita had several of their girlfriends to include Mary at a get-together at her apartment. Later, they all gathered out to the balcony to continue drinking and conversing. One of the ladies in the group decided to sit on the banister and her actions set off a cause for alarm among the group. Moreover, this banister overlooked a huge drop into the yard.

Not wanting this girlfriend to suffer harm, they asked her to get off the banister. Her Parent replied,

"I'm a big girl and can sit here with no problem."

Again, they asked her to get off the banister and she refused. She was adamant about sitting were she wanted.

Rosita, insisted that she get off the banister. This turned into a Parent to Child conversation. Sadly, it ended when the lady said, *"If I can't sit where I want, it is time for me to leave."*

That's the Child: if I can't have my way, then I will take my ball and bat and leave. Rosita said, *"Well I guess it is time for you to leave."*

Consequently, they didn't speak to each other for over a week because of the incident. A way of hooking her Adult would have been: *"We know you are quite comfortable up on the banister, but it is making everyone else around very nervous. So, for the sake of the group, won't you consider coming down?"*

Now, there's no guarantee this approach will work, because, to hook someone's Adult, you have to assume she has an Adult to hook. Remember, most people have very strong Parent and Child ego states, but some never fully develop the Adult.

DO YOU KNOW HOW TO CHANGE A TIRE?

A damsel in distress asks a young man who lives in the same complex as her to change a tire. An Adult question that he answered with his Child ego: *"No I don't know how."*

Clearly, he knew how to change a tire, but his wicked Child kicked in, because he didn't want to be bothered.

This left the damsel speechless. You see, the Adult cannot communicate with the Child. She could have slid into her Child, got mad and told the 28 year old young man lots of derogatory things, but she chose to stay in her Adult and did not respond.

An Adult response on his part would have been: *"Yes, I know how to change a tire, but I prefer not to at this time for whatever reason. Sorry about that."*

Or another could have been: *"Yes, I know how to change a tire. Would you like me to help you?"*

SHOPPING WITH THE WIFE

My Wife and I went to Kmart so she could buy a light yard trimmer which was on sale. She asked my opinion about buying it, however, I didn't answer because she knows how I feel about her working in the yard. We have a person who comes to the house about once every three months to do the trimming, so I was annoyed at why she needed to buy one.

When we arrived at the store, she placed an order at the pharmacy before going to find the trimmers. She found a small trimmer that looked like it would be easy for her to handle. At that time, I had to use the bathroom, so I told her I would be right back and would meet her in the trimmer section.

Upon my return from the restroom, I did not find her. Because the store was so big, I decided to go back to the car to get my phone.

When I came back in the store, I noticed the drinking water was on sale, so I decided to buy six cases of it while I waited for her call. I didn't call her because I knew she was waiting for her medicine at the pharmacy.

When she saw me in the checkout line clearly she was furious. Parent and Child: *"Where were you? I have been looking all over for you. If you didn't want to help me get the trimmer, why didn't you just stay home? You always do this to me. I had to ask strangers to help me find the right kind of line to use with the trimmer and which trimmer was the best."*

On and on she went, easily losing control. *"You said you were going to the bathroom and you never came back."*

She finally walked away from me without giving me a chance to explain.

I took the water to the car and called her. I asked her where she was, and she replied that she was on her way to the car. As soon as she got to the car she wasted zero time to start on me again.

"If you don't want to go shopping with me, just say so. You don't have to run away from me and hide."

Again, I was seeing both her Parent and Child scolding me and doing it while she was angry. At this point, I stopped her and tried to hook her Adult.

I explained to her how I did come back after using the restroom and I didn't see her. So I went to the car to get my telephone in case she tried to call. Not knowing she had to pick out a trim line to go with her trimmer and that she had to wait for her medicine, I tried to make the best use of my time by buying the water. I told her I didn't know what else I could have done except maybe call her first, but because I knew she had to wait at the pharmacy, I thought I was making the right decision.

This did hook her Adult and she was able to see my point of view and cool down. Thank God for the tool, (PAC).

GUILTY

The responsibility of holding the position of a Foreperson is no easy task. Simply said, it is downright tough and tests your ability to agree to disagree.

This was a classic case where it was essential to know how to hook the Adult and make the communication process work.

I was the foreman of a jury that presided over a case involving drug dealers. After hearing and seeing all of the evidence over three days, we went into deliberations. I thought it was going to be a slam dunk because we had video evidence of the transaction. I called for a show of hands to see where everyone stood and was shocked to see we were split down the middle as to guilt or innocence.

After deliberating for two days, we were ten guilty and two not guilty. When I asked the two holdouts why they felt the way they did, they did not give me an Adult or credible answer. Their only reply was they didn't think he was guilty, but could not give a supporting reason as to why.

After the third day, I said, **"I cannot communicate like this."**

That is when I told them about the Parent, Adult, and Child concept. I told them the Child won't answer a simple question. The Child is stubborn for no apparent reason. That finally got a reaction from the two "not guilty" jurors and they started to share their reasoning.

First, they said that the police could have switched the evidence. I said the police were not on trial, and the judge said to just consider the evidence presented. Secondly, they said it would not be the first time the jury couldn't reach a verdict in this case. I asked them how they knew that. They said everyone knew that. I said, "Not true. I didn't know it and the Judge asked us, prior to starting, if anyone had any knowledge of this case. We all answered, "No." Did they lie to the Judge?

That inquiry got their attention. So, again, I asked them to stay in their Adult and only consider the evidence presented to us all as the Judge had instructed. Subsequently, on the fourth day, we finally rendered a unanimous guilty verdict.

PASTOR'S PARENT

By the nature of the position, pastors tend to have a strong Parent, because they teach the Word. A former pastor of mine had an unusually strong Parent and Child that often appeared in the pulpit in an unfortunate manner.

He did things in the pulpit that were humiliating to his wife and awkward for the congregation to witness. His wife was head of the praise and worship portion of the service. Unexpectedly, he would start yelling at his wife while standing before the congregation. That eventually led to their divorce.

He wanted a Parent-to-Child relationship, whereas she wanted an Adult-to-Adult one. When word of their divorce started circulating around the congregation, another member and I took it upon ourselves to confront him. Our goal was to talk to him about the Parent, Adult, and Child to see if it would help his relationship.

He was a man who claimed to hunger and thirst after knowledge—not just spiritual, but secular knowledge as well. He would travel to a conference once a year and come back excited to share what he had learned with anyone who would listen. Case in point: do you know why McDonald's is so successful? It takes the same process and reproduces it in all of their franchises. This helps keep costs under control, makes the food taste the same, and helps the buildings look identical.

He seemed to delight in learning things like that, so I thought he would be a good candidate for the Parent, Adult, and Child concept.

After explaining to him how the PAC tool worked, his response was that it was nonsense. So, I asked him why he yelled at his wife and berated her in front of the congregation. It was the ultimate Parent to Child conversation. His answer bordered on the insane: "Because she deserves it."

Then, he went on to explain that all was okay between him and his wife and they were just fine. He thought things were fine because that was his preferred method of communicating and he didn't see anything wrong with it. His wife felt completely different.

Then I asked him if the rumors about him getting a divorce were true. He said it was not true—he lied (Child). By lying, he hooked my Child, and I got angry and called him a liar. He said he didn't lie, because I hadn't asked the right question. It was a case of the wicked Child playing games.

Shortly after that visit, my family and I left the church. I couldn't continue to be under his leadership knowing how he treated his wife. He tried to convince me to stay in the church because he said how he related to his wife had nothing to do with his ability to minister to the congregation.

I believe this was truly a man of God, inspired by the Holy Spirit to teach and preach the Word of God. The problem was that his Parent and Child got in the way and we could not stand to see him yelling at his wife during a service.

HERE COMES THE DEVIL

After a wonderful praise and worship service and an excellent word from the pulpit, we left the church and got in our car only to have Satan follow us.

Is the phrase "The devil made me do it familiar to you?" Well, this is another version of blaming him for our own shortcomings.

I am paraphrasing another member of my church who related this story to me.

"Let's be real," he started. "I'm going to tell you exactly what happened to me." His son's girlfriend, who went to church with them, wanted to be dropped at a bus stop so she could catch the 12:00 p.m. ferry back to St. John. His wife wanted to stop at the grocery store to do some serious shopping. To accommodate both, he suggested dropping his wife first, dropping Daisy off at the ferry and then going back to pick up his wife. That way Daisy would make the 12:00 p.m. ferry and his wife would have plenty of time to shop. He thought that was a real Adult solution that would satisfy all.

To his disappointment, it hooked his wife's Parent and she said to him, "Just do what Daisy said, and drop her at a bus stop." She said it with a lot of malice and because of that, it hooked his Child. He tried to stay in his Adult and told his wife that Daisy would not make the 12:00 p.m. boat if he just dropped her at a bus stop.

His wife was adamant and said that it wasn't his concern and to just do what he was told.

He became angry and asked his wife what difference it made to her whether he dropped Daisy off at the ferry. The difference, she said, was that Daisy didn't ask to be dropped at the ferry. Before he knew it, they were in a big argument over the silly situation.

He became totally out of control and said, "Okay, you tell me what you want me to do. Tell me everything I should do. Tell me if I should drop her, where I should drop her, how I should drop her, everything." They were both very upset and bent out of shape. This is why I said in the beginning, 'Here comes the Devil.'

"I submit to you it was not the Devil but, instead, a lack of knowledge about how to communicate." After making his initial declaration in his Adult about what he intended to do—only to hear his wife respond in her Parent telling him what to do—He had two choices to avoid an argument. He could hook her Adult by pointing out the practicality of his suggestion, or if that didn't work, just remain silent (the Adult cannot communicate with the Parent or Child) and drop Daisy at a bus stop."

CONVERSATION WITH GOD

I was laying on a gurney in the hospital, waiting to have an operation on my knee when this conversation started:

I said, **"God, what do you think about me being here, getting ready to have this operation?"**

He said, **"You know what I think."**

I said, **"You are not happy about this are you?"**

He said, **"You see, I told you, you know what I think."**

"Why aren't you happy about me having this surgery?"

He said, **"You know why I am not happy."**

"Are you saying it is because you sent your Word to heal me?"

"That's right."

"So, you're saying I am already healed?"

He shrugged. I said, **"Lord, come on, do you expect me to just get up and walk out of the hospital at this point, moments before I am about to have this operation?"**

He said, **"You already know what I want you to do. The real question is are you going to do it?"**

At that point, I said, **"Okay, God, I don't want to talk anymore."** (Adult to Adult).

After a few hours, I woke up in the recovery room. The doctor told me he didn't find anything wrong with my knee.

"What about the MRI and the X-rays that all indicated I had a torn meniscus?"

He said, "I know, but when I went inside the knee, everything was perfect. I don't understand what happened".

My mind went back to the conversation I had with God and how he had said he sent his Word to heal me.

God has a very strong Adult.

HERE COMES THE JUDGE

Judges have strong Parent and Child ego states by the nature of their profession.

Louis was remodeling a bathroom for a judge's ex-wife. After the Judge went with Louis to buy all the materials for the job, Louis's wife became very ill. The severity of his wife illness was not apparent at the time Louis had agreed to do the remodeling job. It became apparent that her illness was time consuming and quickly became his focus. He could barely balance his regular job, kids, much less his wife's illness.

He tried to call the Judge to update him on the situation and when he couldn't get through, he left messages. Because he left messages, the Judge knew about Louis' unfortunate situation.

Still, the Judge (in his Parent) wrote a scathing letter which he sent by certified mail to Louis, stating he wanted back the money he spent for the materials within thirty days for breach of contract.

Keep in mind, the Judge had the materials and wanted the money. The letter could not have come at a worse time because Louis' wife was in the hospital having surgery. This is a classic example of an appalling Parent trying to bully a Child.

The Adult would have picked up the phone and talked Adult to Adult about the situation instead of writing and sending a certified letter.

When Louis got the letter from the Judge, it immediately hooked his Child, and he obeyed.

The situation created animosity between Louis' wife and the Judge. After all, they were family.

"Why didn't you just call?"

He, the Judge, later said the money was not important. He just felt disrespected and wanted to drive his point home. The Child felt disrespected.

JUDGE

His method of handling a misunderstanding with his mate was to lock her out of the house. Who does that? (A terrible Child.)

Again, this is normal with someone who has a strong Parent and Child. An Adult would never behave in such a manner.

On several occasions, the Judge had locked his significant other out of the house. Again, who does that? (The wicked Child.)

MY FATHER-IN-LAW

After spending thirty-something years in the military, it is easy to see how my father-in-law could develop such a strong Parent and Child. He is accustomed to others obeying him without question. They just follow orders or suffer the consequences. When someone didn't obey him, he would get very upset and start yelling just to make his point.

Although he has become more calm and relaxed over the years, he still has his moments. Whenever my wife went to visit him in Puerto Rico, for any length of time, she would regrettably come home sad and frustrated because of the way he treated her. He wants a Parent to Child relationship and she cannot tolerate that form of communication with him. She always comes back home, declaring she will never go to see him again. She takes it personally when he yells at her because he doesn't yell at her brothers.

When I talked to him about the situation, his response was, "It's just the way I am."

"I know, but it doesn't mean you cannot change," I replied.

"It is very difficult, at age seventy-nine, to learn new ways to communicate, especially when I was never much of a reader." (Remember, the Adult is best developed through reading and experiences that lead to wisdom.)

My father-in-law is the first person to say he wished he could read, but every time he tried he would fall asleep. His problem of falling asleep goes back to when he was in school. Unfortunately, he is convinced that reading will never be a part of his life.

That is okay. Remember, there are other ways to learn. You can listen and learn quite well. But you have to be humble and willing to learn something new.

You cannot revert to the notion that you are too old to change or too set in your old, stubborn ways.

Learn this concept about the Parent, Adult, and Child, and it will set you free. He is changing little by little.

MY MOTHER-IN-LAW

My mother-in-law had a strong Child. She often cried and played the victim role of "Nobody loves me."

She communicated with her husband Child to Parent for many years. He is ex-military and the relationship worked just fine for years, until she decided to develop her Adult and things changed.

She suddenly started to talk to him Adult to Adult and the result was a better relationship. For a while, he treated his children differently and life was more relaxed in their household. Sometimes in the heat of battle, they had a tendency to revert to their old way of communicating: Child to Child or Child to Parent. This is natural if you don't know how the tool of Parent, Adult, and Child works and how to apply them on a regular basis.

Last month, my mother in law's sister died of a broken heart, both figuratively and literally. Obese and unable to take care of herself, she discovered that no one wanted to be bothered with her wellbeing. Her children didn't have the time nor inclination to step up and do what was necessary to give her peace of mind. She went from home to home trying to find love and comfort only to end up sad, depressed and alone.

My mother-in-law stepped up for seven years. She took her sister into her home and cared for her, but the wear and tear on her own body finally took its toll. The Adult in my mother-in-law had to make some hard decisions. That is when the family asked the sister's daughter to take care of her. Reluctantly, she agreed but the mother and daughter were not happy with the arrangement.

This hooked my mother in law's Child and she became very emotional over how her sister was treated. The Adult showed up in the form of her brother, who made the choice to put his sister in a home-care facility. But it was too little too late.

HONOR YOUR FATHER AND MOTHER AND YOU SHALL HAVE LONG LIFE

"Honor your father and mother," which is the first commandment with promise, "that it may be well with you and you may live long on the earth" (Ephesians 6:2-3).

My parents had very strong Parent and Child personalities. They both drank a lot, so they were drunk and argued most of the time (Child). When they were drunk they were different people. They would fight with each other and other people, such as my Aunt and Uncle. When they were sober, the Parent would emerge: ***"Get up."***

"Go to school." "Wash the dishes."
"Go to bed."
"Eat all your food."
"Stop playing around."
"Be quiet." "Do your homework."

And so forth and so on they would continue with their [Parent].

My father was very smart—he read all the time, mostly for pleasure. He had a strong Adult; unfortunately, he never shared his knowledge with me. This is not true. He did teach me an invaluable lesson about gambling. The very first paycheck I ever received I lost to him in a poker game. Afterwards I said, okay Dad, give me back my money [Child]. He answered in his [Adult], if you can't afford to lose, do not gamble. My dad gave me two things that day, enough money for bus fare the following week to go to work and a lesson I never forgot about gambling.

He would always talk at me, but not to me.

I don't remember ever having an Adult conversation with my father. The closest we ever came was when I was just finding out about women sexually. I was nineteen at the time. I was dating seriously for the first time, and the advice he gave me was, "You'd better know what comes out of your penis when you are having sex, before you get yourself in trouble."

Unfortunately, I didn't know and I ended up getting a woman pregnant.

After my father passed away, my mother cut way down on her drinking. That is when I started seeing more of her Adult. I was living in the Virgin Islands at the time, so it was a long-distance relationship. Nevertheless, it was very good to see that wonderful change in her.

My parents were wonderful people, but they were also a product of the life and times in which they lived, when drinking and smoking were the norm.

My father taught (Parent) me how to read, and I've been reading ever since. I learned from observing him.

My mother taught (Parent) me the truth about God. I have become a better person because she showed me how to have a relationship with Him. She bought me my first Bible. I first learned to love God because she loved God. I learned to love God because she first loved me.

We love each other because he loved us first.
(1John 4:19)

WHATEVER YOU DO TO THE LEAST OF THEM, YOU HAVE DONE UNTO ME!

"And the King will say, 'I tell you the truth, when you did it to one of the least of these my brothers and sisters, you were doing it to me!" (Matthew 25:40)

As a young teenager, about fourteen, a man approached me in a restroom at a movie theater while I was urinating. The man said, "Hey, what is that?" And he reached out to touch my penis. That freaked me out and I immediately stopped urinating. I zipped up my pants and left the bathroom.

When that happened to me, it hooked my Child—big time. Going forward, I noticed whenever I was trying to urinate in the company of other males I had trouble. My stomach muscles would automatically tighten up and would not let me urinate. My emotions (scared Child) took over, rendering me incapable of doing the simplest function of urinating in front of other men.

Years later, when I found out about the Parent, Adult, Child, I was able to use the concept to begin my healing.

My Adult was able to analyze what had happened to me and I was able to put things in their proper perspective. The incident had a profound effect on my Child because it was foreign to me. Consequently, my body would shut down every time I was in that situation. Later, my Adult stepped in and said it was okay to urinate in front of other men. Not everyone is a pervert. I decided that one crazy person would not dictate the rest of my life. It was not easy to get over that phobia, but my Adult prevailed and I am a happier man.

I used the technique that the Adult cannot communicate with the Child, so I was able to put what happened behind me.

AS A MAN THINKS—SO IS HE

If a man does not change the way he thinks, that man will never change. This technique of Parent, Adult, and Child is all about the way we think when we speak to each other. You are either coming from one or the other ego states when you converse.

One day in church, the pastor was so grateful in his praising God that it moved him to tears. He literally fell to his knees while in the pulpit and started crying and praising God at the same time. He was in his Child (emotional) and sincere in what he was doing. After a considerable amount of time, he switched to his Parent and started teaching the Word of God. Remember, the Parent and Child go hand-in-hand. It is also important to remember that there is nothing wrong with any of these ego states; the important thing is just to identify which state is operating at any given time.

Albert Einstein said, "The definition of crazy is doing the same thing over and over again and expecting a different result." This tool gives you the opportunity to come up with a new approach to solve an old problem: communication.

BLOCKING TRAFFIC

This is a classic case of the wicked Child.

As my wife left the fabric store to continue with her daily errands, she noticed a car had blocked her in. The ignorant driver had left his car in the middle of the road to go into a convenience store. My wife blew her horn, seeking the driver to move his car.

"No," he said, "just wait."

My wife told the man she couldn't wait and asked the man again to please move his car immediately.

He started using bad words and my wife realized what she was dealing with (wicked Child). She didn't say another word. Instead, she picked up her cell phone and called the police.

MAKING LOVE

Adult Conversation with Myself.

Forty years ago I read a book called **Total Orgasm**. I thought it was about sex, but it was about control. The book demonstrated how to have an internal dialogue about controlling your feelings (Child). The Adult is focused on control and the Child is focused on feelings. What I learned from the book was that, by controlling my breathing, I could control how I felt and, therefore, have a complete orgasm, instead of a local one felt only in the groin area.

An experienced runner might exhibit the same kind of control while running. The ability to keep your breathing under control helps to prevent your emotions from running wild (no pun intended). Total orgasm is referring to the whole body enjoying the climax sensation. According to the book, by talking to yourself, you can send the sensations you are feeling (Child) to your toes, feet, hands, arms, legs, neck, and so forth, simply by letting your Adult stay in control. The Adult will control his feelings by controlling the way he breathes. Conversely, if you can control your breathing, you can control how you feel.

Remember, feelings are part of the Child. If I want to control how I feel (Child), I control my breathing. I let my Adult take charge and dictate how my body will react.

The results are usually both parties enjoy a more satisfying and complete experience.

MOM, ARE YOU UPSET ABOUT SOMETHING?

I was playing with my sister and unintentionally did something to set her off. I hooked her Child—big time—and, try as I did, I could not bring her out of it.

It happened when we were both teenagers. We were the only ones at home. She started screaming for what I considered an insignificant reason.

"Mary, stop screaming or I will give you a real reason to scream (Parent)!"

She kept right on screaming, ignoring my warning.

"Okay, Mary." Again, I begged her to stop screaming. It was so loud that I thought the neighbors would call the police. Well, she didn't stop, so I hit her to make her stop. She hooked my Parent, and I was now imposing my will to make her stop. Hitting her only intensified her screaming and she was totally out of control. If, in the beginning, the screaming was only for show, it was then for real.

So, I doubled my efforts and finally, she realized I was serious, and she stopped screaming.

I left the house thinking I showed her who was boss (Parent).

Hours later, when I walked through my front door, something told me to duck (Holy Spirit). When I looked, a bat hit the door where my head was.

"Mom, are you upset about something?"

She said, "Don't you ever put your hands on my daughter again!"

I tried to stay calm (Adult) and explain to her what had happened. She knew how Mary could be, so it worked because she understood how Mary left me little choice. Still, she made her point to me about never putting my hands on my sister.

Mary's Child was in control when she was screaming, and I tried, at first, to use my Adult by talking to her, trying to make her understand that she had to stop screaming. When she didn't, it hooked my Parent, (Parent-to-Child conversation) and I beat her, thinking it was the only way to make her shut up.

I didn't have the tool [PAC] at my command to manage the situation better.

FOURSOME

I play golf with a foursome that consists of two lawyers and a doctor. One of the lawyers, Peter, has such a strong Parent that it makes playing golf more provocative than fun. He is a difficult person to be around and he knows it. (He knows it but he doesn't want to change.) He has made statements like: ***"Look, I know I'm disgusting but that is the way I am."***

One particular day, I hit a golf ball down the left side of the fairway and Peter and Luke drove to my ball with their cart. Luke was all set to hit my ball when I yelled from across the fairway, "Stop! Don't hit that ball; it's mine."

Peter said to me, "Don't you think he knows his own ball?"

"I don't know what he knows." So I drove up to the ball and identified it as my ball. Instead of Peter apologizing like an Adult, he stayed in his Parent and said, "Well, you should have let him hit it anyway and incur a two-stroke penalty for hitting the wrong ball."

Peter's strong Parent didn't allow him to admit that he was wrong.

I just shook my head in disbelief. I knew that was his nature, and, unless he decides to change (Adult) the way he thinks, he will never change his behavior.

PETER

I see a change.

Yesterday, while we were playing golf, a situation arose about a rule in golf. When we asked Peter about the ruling, he started to yell out the answer (Parent). On top of that, he was upset (Child) because we questioned him about his interpretation of the rule.

So, I calmly (Adult) called him over to the spot in question, and he, to his credit, told the other golfer not to hit the ball until he had a better look at the situation. Then, in a calm Adult manner, he explained why the rule applied and provided the options as to how he could play the ball.

He even went as far as to say he was willing to bend the rules that one time to give the golfer relief. That is something he would have never done before. The golfer played the ball from its position, but the important thing is that Peter showed flexibility. Something he rarely did.

I was able to hook his Adult—something that wasn't easy—and he acted accordingly.

DON'T LET THE SUN GO DOWN ON YOUR ANGER

I was talking to my wife about something that I can't even remember because the conversation took place about seventeen years ago. While we were talking, she said something that hooked my Child, and I got angry. I started yelling at her and she was yelling back. I don't ever remember being so upset with my wife and I really lost control.

The louder and more boisterous I became, the worse the situation grew. At that moment, my son, who was about ten at the time, stepped right in between us and told me to stop yelling at his mother. He instantaneously hooked my Adult, and I stopped.

All it took was one mature voice to see the error of my ways and I just walked away.

That night, I apologized to my wife. I didn't want to go to sleep with it on my mind.

The argument was over and forgotten.

DON'T LET ANYONE ELSE DRIVE MY CAR

My sister and her girlfriend came to St. Thomas for vacation and needed transportation during their stay. I was leaving the island for a few days, so I offered her my car.

"Just don't let anyone else drive it," I told her (Parent).

When I returned, I discovered she had let her girlfriend drive my car and I got angry (Child).

I started yelling (Parent), "Didn't I tell you not to let anyone else drive the car?"

"I know," she said, "but I don't really know how to drive a standard-transmission car."

To my sister's credit, she stayed in her Adult and explained to me the reason she let her girlfriend drive. She said, "I was stuck on a hill and probably would have burned out your clutch if I hadn't let her drive."

That simple statement hooked my Adult and I understood completely why she had let her girlfriend drive my car.

I apologized to her for getting angry without even listening to her side.

"You did the right thing," I said.

My sister displayed an amazing Adult quality in the midst of my Childish outburst.

MY BROTHER-IN-LAW

"Bobby, every time I hit the golf ball, it goes to the right. Can you tell me why?"

"Thomas, let's go to the range to see what's going on. I am not the best person to give advice, especially with an average golf score of about one hundred, but let's take a look at your swing anyway."

After watching his swing, I really couldn't put my finger on why his balls went to the right. However, I came across a video called "The Secret of Golf," and I thought it was great. It explained the golf club in detail and how to use it as a tool to make the ball do what you want.

I sent the video to Thomas because it addressed the exact issue he was complaining about. However, because I had mentioned to him that my game hadn't shown an immediate improvement, he refused to watch it.

That was his Child—his stubborn Child.

"How do you know if the techniques will or will not work if you don't even watch and try to learn?"

His refusal to watch the video hinged on the fact that, if it didn't help me, how could it help him.

The Adult would have, at least, looked at the video and made an informed decision based on what he had seen and possibly learned.

"Come on, man. Watch the video."

PASSING IT ON

My daughter, Martha, called me one Saturday morning just to talk. Sensing something was on her mind, I started probing her with questions.

"How are you doing on your job? Is everything okay with my grandkids?"

She started opening up to me and told me about her work and problems with the different personalities. She was perplexed because she wasn't sure how to deal with everyone and all their different idiosyncrasies. I offered my advice.

I explained the Parent, Adult, Child techniques to her, and she loved it. I told her how everyone has a Parent, Adult, and Child and how each of these psychological states work.

The Parent gives advice, directions, commands, guidance, and so forth and so on.

The Child has all the emotions, such as fear, happiness, anger, love, peace, and so forth.

The Adult is the one who reasons, negotiates, and talks in a rational manner and is teachable, trainable, understanding and wise, just to name a few.

The Adult generally knows how to hook the Adult in another person. My daughter was so excited about this tool, especially after I gave her a few examples of how it worked.

"How come you never told me about this before?" She asked. The tool made perfect sense to her and she wanted more.

So, I am passing it on. To everyone who wants a better understanding of the different psychological states and how to learn to reason and communicate with each other, here it is.

The concepts [PAC] are universal and simple in their application and understanding.

RIDING TO WORK

I picked up my daughter Abigail and her husband, Daniel, to give them a ride to work. The first thing I noticed when they got into the car was how quiet it was. Evidently, they had fought and weren't speaking to each other.

After a few miles, I couldn't take the silence anymore, so I started telling them about the Parent, Adult, and Child. The Child gets angry and stops talking and, obviously, they were both in their Child at that moment.

I explained how the Child can communicate in this manner indefinitely, especially without a tool to bring him or her out of the Child ego state.

I never asked them what they were arguing about. It didn't matter.

Later that day, Daniel called me to say thanks. He said it worked. Without knowing what the issue was, I was able to help them solve their communication problem just by explaining the tool. It works!

WORSE, IT'S MILLI!

The whole family was in Washington, DC for Warren's, wedding. He is my brother. Milli is my oldest sister and has a strong Parent. When we were young, she had to babysit me and my five siblings on a regular basis, so she had ample opportunity to develop the Parent. On the night prior to my brother's wedding, we were all acting the fool (Child) at a big bachelor party that was quickly getting out of control. We were staying at a motel in a residential part of town. We were having a lot of fun, but it was very noisy. Everyone was drinking and smoking marijuana when there suddenly came a loud banging on the door.

Somebody yelled, "Oh lord; it's the police."

Then Buzzy Ward, a good friend from the Hood, looked outside and said, "No, it's not the police. It's worse; it's Milli."

We all got really scared (Child). Milli (Parent) had that effect on us.

HAIRCUT

"Robert, don't come home today without a haircut (Parent). Here is twenty dollars so you don't have an excuse not to cut your hair."

Later that day when I saw he hadn't cut his hair, I was angry (Child). "What happened?"

He said he didn't want to cut his hair.

"It is not an option. You cut your hair or else!"

Again, the next day I told him not to come home without cutting his hair. Defiantly, he came home again without doing what I had told him to do. I was livid and ready to go to battle with him over the issue. To his credit, he tried to hook my Adult by explaining how he was obedient in all things pertaining to home, school, his behavior in the streets, and so forth, but in that one case, all he wanted to do was to grow his hair.

"Is that so bad?" he asked.

It didn't work. I was still in my Child and more irate than ever. "You need to cut your hair because it looks unkempt and unsanitary." I then succeeded in hooking his Child and he also became angry.

We continued yelling at each other until it escalated into pushing and shoving, and I had him up against the wall. At that very moment, my wife walked into the room and broke the spell just long enough for me to catch myself. I immediately walked out of the room, thinking, ***do you really want to fight with your son over a haircut?***

The answer was easy. No, I did not want to have a physical fight with him, but I needed a solution to the dilemma and I needed it immediately. I went into another room and asked God for help. I said, "Please give me a solution to this problem right here and now. I don't want this to drag into another day. Give me an answer now."

And God said, **"Get a mediator."**

That instantaneously hooked my Adult so I went back to my son, and told him what I had in mind. He was in full agreement, so I asked him who he thought could mediate this crisis. After we offered up a few names, we finally hit one that we both agreed on. The person was a police officer that we both knew and respected.

The next day, all three of us sat in an office to discuss a solution to the hair crisis. I started by saying that I loved my son and he was a good kid, but I didn't like his long hair. However, as long as he lived under my roof he would have to obey (Parent).

My son countered by saying that he did everything I asked of him, but in that one area, he didn't want to obey. The police officer said to me, "I've heard both sides. We, as police officers, do not judge kids by the length of their hair. What police look for in teenagers is whether they are wearing colors that represent a gang. Have they been in trouble with the law and do they carry weapons?"

So, he said as long as Robert didn't belong to any gang, he was cool as far as the police were concerned. Then he turned to my son and said, in reference to living under my roof, that he had a responsibility to listen and obey his mother and father.

In the end, I relinquished and let him keep his hair. The discussion with the police officer hooked my Adult and I was able to have a different outlook.

About six months later, my son cut his hair of his own accord. More importantly, we were able to maintain a normal family relationship after we overcame the disagreement.

HOW NOT TO TREAT A LADY

Frances has been seeing a man for the better part of five years. The relationship has been unstable, at best. The guy has a peculiar habit of dropping off the radar for days or even weeks at a time.

Case in point: they had a date and he had to pick her up at a specific time and place. She was dressed and ready to go but he never showed up or called.

The very next day, they had planned to go out to a family gathering and again, she did not hear from him. On the third day, she received a text message from him saying he was sick. Evidently, on Saturday, he was in his car on the way to her house when he didn't feel well so he turned around and went back home, without calling her or sending any notification.

Who does that? The Child. Only the inconsiderate Child would do that. An Adult would pick up the phone and call his girlfriend to let her know what was going on. Instead, he let her worry and wonder for three days as to his whereabouts.

On top of all that, the text he sent on the third day was the only communication he had with her for the entire month that followed the incidents.

Who does that?

Over the last five years, he had a habit of dropping off the grid without warning on several occasions. If nothing else, it's disconcerting and inconsiderate. His actions are selfish, which is part of the Child. It is not possible for an Adult to have a relationship with a Child. I am not surprised she is not talking to him anymore.

The Adult cannot communicate with the Child.

THE HAIRPIECE

My wife and I witnessed my sister and her husband acting out in their Child over my sister's wig. We were in an upscale restaurant in downtown Annapolis, Md, when Thomas noticed Eve's wig.

"What's that on your head?" he asked.

"Shut up, Thomas, and leave me alone."

"Eve, take that thing off your head. You look ridiculous."

"Shut up, and leave me alone."

Eve, getting angry (Child), actually grabbed a knife off the table and threatened Thomas. Thomas ignored the knife and continued his insults about her wig.

"Eve, if you don't take that off your head, I will!" (Parent.)

My wife and I were a little alarmed because they both had been drinking, and that's an automatic hook on the [Child] emotions. At that point, we did not know how the thing was going to play out, but, in the end, Eve kept on her wig and Thomas enjoyed his continuous insults.

Again, this is a perfect illustration of how the Child and Parent and/or the Child and Child can communicate indefinitely.

BULLFOOT

Paul and Simeon have been visiting the Virgin Islands for vacation for the past twenty years. I receive their company with mixed emotions because they both have a strong Parent and Child.

For instance, take Simeon he likes to tell people what to do (Parent). He is always giving commands and instructions. He uses the fact that he has bad ankles and feet to justify his ways. When he starts with his Parent—give me this, and do that for me—it hooks my Child and I get upset. I tell him I don't like to be told to wait on him, and he says, "But I am on crutches; what can I do?"

But, if the truth is told, he was always like that. I never saw an effort from him to develop his Adult. He uses phrases like, "Just be you or be real," but they are like moving targets always changing.

Simeon likes to argue about anything. This is normal behavior for a person with a strong Child and Parent. Simeon told me the last book he read was **Iceberg Slim** and that was forty-something years ago. In my opinion, it is very difficult to develop the Adult without reading and having experiences that lead to wisdom. Paul, on the other hand, has come a long way over the past year. Before that (and still on occasions) these two always converse Child to Child, arguing and fighting all the time, or Parent to Parent, trying to tell each other what to do or how to act.

In the last year, I've noticed Paul has made subtle changes in his life. He's stopped drinking and doesn't use profanity anymore. He lacks the desire to go to strip clubs as was the case in the past. Most importantly, he has accepted Jesus Christ as his Lord and Savior and goes to church on a regular basis.

After church, he wants to talk about the sermon and has a genuine interest in God's Word. In his thirst for knowledge of God's Word, he is developing his Adult. It is an important beginning in his growth as a person with a stronger Adult.

The common thread is they have known each other all their lives, but the Adult cannot communicate continuously with the Child or Parent. I see it happening now, when Simeon starts with his Parent, I notice Paul's reaction is to stay quiet.

RAISE

I asked my boss for a raise and his response was (Parent), **"Do you think you deserve one?"**

I tried to stay in my Adult: **"Don't ask me that question."**

It worked. I hooked his Adult. "Okay, he said, **I was just joking.** They haven't given me the authorization to give out raises yet, but when they do, you will get one."

SINGLE MOTHER

Being a single mother is without question the hardest job in the whole world because another life depends on you and you don't have anyone to rely on or a manual with instructions.

A thirty seven year old mother with two boys, fourteen and eleven, will challenge any Parent's and Child's sanity. A single mother, not having the Parent, Adult, and Child tool as a guide to navigate one's way, makes life that much harder.

Carole has been a single parent for the past fourteen years and it hasn't been easy. Carole grew up in a culture where punishment was swift and cruel. On several occasions, punishment went to the extreme like the time she witnessed a neighbor tied naked to a tree in front of her house for lying to her mother. In her culture, there were no boundaries on punishment. Parents would burn their children, make them crawl on hot cement, and humiliate them in front of neighbors and friends.

Fast forward to where we find her now. She is a mother of two teenage boys and it's difficult for her to break the cycle of her culture. When Carole dishes out punishment she is usually in her Child. She is very angry and uses her hands to beat them. She never plans to hurt them, just teach them right from wrong. She has a very strong Parent and Child. Carole doesn't have a lot of patience with her boys. When she speaks, if they don't respond immediately, she will curse and start beating them right away. The fact that she is a school teacher reinforces her Parent and Child.

One day I was walking by her window when I overheard her interacting with her children. The bad words she used shocked me. I didn't know she could use profanity like she did. Later that day, I asked her about it. She said, Robert, if you had to deal with these two boys every day, you also would be saying a lot of swear words. I asked her if she ever tried to talk to them in her (Adult.) She replied "Yes," until I get sick of talking to them nicely. When I can't stand to be nice anymore I just tell them exactly how I feel and I don't care what comes out of my mouth."

Ricky, her oldest son, is a character to be reckoned with. He has a very strong and difficult Child ego. When he is confronted with a situation that is disagreeable to him, his defense mechanism is to shut his mouth and just stare at you. He may cry and without making a sound, tears will run down his cheek. When he is in his Child ego, it is impossible to talk to him. While trying to talk to him, he just remains silent with this vacant stare on his face. The stare is very disconcerting. One has to wonder what is going on inside his head because, try as we might, we can't get him to talk when he is in his stubborn Child. On several occasions, when he was like this, I tried changing the subject and talked to him about an unrelated subject. I got a word or two in response, but it didn't last long enough to have a conversation. He needs help. I do believe my book may be of some benefit to him. He reads and is very smart for his age and because of this fact, I think it is possible to hook his Adult.

Imagine, if you will, the mother is yelling and the son is staring. Communication is non-existent. She will lose patience and beat him into submission, but that will never be an acceptable solution with permanent results. How do you bridge the gap between communicating Child to Child and moving to Adult to Adult? They both have to learn how this tool works. Carole, perhaps, must learn to be patient long enough to forge a relationship that excludes the Parent and Child. Talk to your son like you would want an Adult to talk to you.

Ricky said he would prefer to be talked to like an Adult rather than to be yelled at like a Child.

Carole has calmed down over the past year, but her anger is still apparent in her body language. She wants to do better in her relationship with her son, but it's a constant battle between her experiences growing up and learning the new concepts from the (PAC) tool.

FRUSTRATION ON THE JOB

Being a good boss includes more than having the ability to get the job done. How you interact with your subordinates is also important.

Respect for the individual has always been a hallmark of great companies. I believe having this attitude towards its employees is the reason they are great companies to work for.

Joel was recently promoted to a supervisory position. He had both the time and qualifications for the promotion. His ability to get the job done was outstanding, however, his skills in communicating with his subordinates needed some polishing. Joel has a very strong Parent. His approach is to command and control his workers to a fault. Example: "Hey I need you guys to work overtime tonight." Instead of: Hey guys, there is still the job to complete so can you guys work overtime?

When you treat people with respect, (Adult to Adult) they have a tendency to want to do more for you.

When Joel, in his Parent, starts issuing commands and his subordinates don't respond the way he expects, he gets angry (Child) and threatens his subordinates. Example: "If you don't want to work the overtime, maybe I don't need you around because there are plenty of folks who would like your job."

It's the Parent that commands and the Child that threatens, but the Adult will find a way to talk to you and get better results.

Another example of his Parent being in control came out when he was conducting a chess tournament for kids. One particular game was going on forever so he put five minutes on the clock for each child. Joel told the youngsters, "When your time expires, the game is over." His instructions were clear and simple, or so we thought. However, when one of the kid's time expired instead of the game being over, Joel came up with a new rule. Joel said, "The child with time still on his clock must declare himself the winner." Where did this rule come from? I asked Joel what was going on and his reply was that it's the rules of Chess. I said this is the first time the kids ever played with a clock and you didn't mention that part of the rule when you gave them five minutes each. He said, (Parent) the rules are the rules and that's how I am running this tournament. His Parent was so strong that he would not listen to Adult reasoning and just insisted that the rules were the rules and cannot be changed. The impact of his decision caused the game to be a draw. One kid clearly should have won.

When I saw him acting like this, I knew his inability to change was ignorance of not having the (Parent, Adult, and Child) tool.

This tool, (PAC) once understood properly, applies to all aspects of life, whether it's working, playing, entertaining or just socializing.

Joel would have a better working environment if he took the time to learn about the Parent, Adult, and Child tool.

As a laborer you also have certain responsibilities. You get paid to do a job. It's too bad if you don't like the way your supervisor talks to you. That is your (Child) that doesn't like the way he talks to you. Your Adult would say, "Okay, so he needs me to do this or that, so I will overlook how he tells me and just do it."

Complaining about how your boss talks to you doesn't help. Thinking that he is picking on you should be of no consequence as to the way you do your job. The Bottom line is you have a job to do. The Adult in you should keep that in focus. It's your job to be on time every day, ready and prepared to work, staying and working until the last minute, and not stopping five or ten minutes before the shift is finished. Whatever it takes, do your job with a positive attitude that shows you appreciate the opportunity you have been given.

In closing, I encourage the laborer to keep developing the Parent, Adult, and Child tool in his being and use it when talking to a supervisor.

We can't always control how people talk to us but we can control our reaction to what they say. Stay in your Adult!

THREE HUNDRED AND SIXTY DEGREES

For there is no respect of persons with God (Romans 2:11).

The following is a synopsis of my life. The (Parent, Adult and Child) tool remains one of the important factors in turning my life around. While heading down the path of total destruction, this tool helped save me. I am telling my story to show how this tool worked for me. Hopefully, it will work for countless others also.

I started out with an uncompromising faith in God. As a young person, I hungered and thirsted for Him all the time. I would put my faith in Him, never questioning the outcome. I was always seeking different ways for Him to reveal His presence to me. Once I said, "God, make it rain if this is the way you want me to handle a certain situation." Out of the clear blue, it rained.

I would go about this in simple things like the time I needed a bottle opener. I saw a handle in a cup holder and as I pulled it out, I said, "This is a bottle opener." And, presto, it was. Just as I spoke it, it happened.

I would ask Him to reveal Himself in every situation in which I found myself. Then He would show up all the time with signs and wonders that literally startled me. I expected the result He produced, but was still amazed when God did it.

I remember, at the tender age of about ten, the only thing I wanted for Christmas was a Bible. My goal was to learn all I could about this awesome person called Jesus.

As it happened, I started to give more influence to my sin nature because of the negative influence of friends and family.

We, as young teenagers, did stupid things like the time we were going to the park to play ball. When we got there, we saw a car with a big, black Doberman Pinscher in it. My cousin decided to agitate and harass the dog. We were in our early teens and my cousin was the oldest.

Several white kids, including the owner of the dog, were irritated.

"Hey, get away from my car and dog. If you want to play with him, how about if I let him loose and see what happens?"

There were about eight of them and only six of us. My cousin, who has never backed down from a challenge, turned to me and said, "Run home and tell Rebecca to give you my gun."

I saw the impending danger developing, so I didn't hesitate to follow his instruction. When I returned, they were still in a heated argument. I slipped the gun to James. One of the members of the other group saw the transaction and told their leader that we had a gun. The leader said, "You can't take us all out with just one gun." And James said, "You're right, but I know for sure I will take you out."

Once the gun was introduced into the mix, things quickly abated. After that, everybody went his own way. We were very fortunate because it could have ended in tragedy.

This is a clear case of not knowing about the tool, (PAC).

* * *

From my early beginning of hunger and thirst for God, I changed, I started developing my sin nature like never before. I went on a rampage of drunken behavior that lasted well past my teenage years.

One particular Saturday night, we were all drinking and looking for some mischief to get into. About ten of us walked down Massachusetts Avenue in Cambridge, Massachusetts, toward Harvard Square where we saw a man with a gorgeous woman.

"Hey, your woman sure is fine," we said.

We started with taunts and it escalated into disrespectful slurs. The gentleman told us to behave. Now, I must remind you, there were ten of us, and he continued walking like it was no big deal to be taunted by ten black teenagers.

When we wouldn't let up, he told his girlfriend to keep going while he dealt with us. He walked into an alley and motioned us to follow.

We were right behind him telling him all the things we were going to do to him.

Once in the alley, we formed a circle around him. I remembered how cool and relaxed he seemed. We were egging each other on trying to convince each other to take the first leap at the guy, but nobody did.

After babbling back and forth in that manner for several minutes, we reckoned it was in our best interest to just let him go. He coolly walked out from the midst of us to join his girlfriend who didn't seem a bit concerned about our shenanigans.

Personally, in retrospect I think we were lucky he decided to let us walk away.

* * *

While cultivating my sin nature, I decided to try something stronger than liquor. Cough medicine became one of my favorite highs, back in the day. I would walk into the pharmacy and buy *Robitussin* DM cough syrup and drink the whole bottle in one sitting. That would cause me to go into such a heavy "nod" that it was only by the Grace of God I was able to recover. Clearly, a heroin addict had nothing on me.

When I was in a deep nod, it was like a dream. I could hear people like my daughter talking to me, asking if I was sleepy, and I couldn't respond. Imagine drinking, driving, and taking cough medicine. I was playing with a deadly combination.

Thank God, in the midst of all my foolishness, I still had a decent head on my shoulders.

From early in life, I knew I wanted to have a job where I could dress up and look nice. I wanted to work with my hands, not in an office or factory, but in the field. After high school, I was lying in bed one morning and didn't want to get up to go to work. My mother gave me a choice, of either I would go to work or join the military. At the recruiter's office, the recruiter told me that I had to score an eighty percent or better to qualify for electronics. Back in 1969, I knew electronics would be the wave of the future and so I decided to roll the proverbial dice. While I was taking the test, time expired before I could finish and the sergeant gave me a break by leaving the room to get coffee. I quickly turned to the math section and finished answering the questions that I knew. The extra time allowed me to finish. When the results came back, I had scored an exact eighty percent.

I passed, but that was just the first hurdle. I was the only black candidate in a class of over one hundred and fifty students who were studying electronics. The course was one year long, with exams every two weeks. If we failed any two consecutive weeks we were out, and they could send us to any school they wanted: military police, cooking, artillery, administration, and so on.

I worked extra hard because I wanted that future, and I felt that because of the way I qualified, I had to prove to myself I could do the work.

Twelve months later I graduated from the program called Inertial Navigation and Radar Repair.

Shortly after school, my orders were for Japan to work on the F14 Phantom jet. It was the most advanced plane of its time in the Air Force. I repaired the navigation system for that plane. I think I had the best job an enlisted man could have in the Air Force.

Outside of work, I still carried on like I had no sense—high most of the time on speed, from pills called black beauties. They would keep me going for twenty-four hours at a time. In addition to that, my friends and I would stand around in a group and drink a whole bottle of vodka in one sitting. In just ten or fifteen minutes, the bottle would be finished.

Only the mercy of God brought me through those years in the Air Force.

I had no knowledge of how to control the wicked Child.

* * *

On returning to the States after my enlistment, I came home to a family of two wonderful children and a wife. Because of my immaturity and drunken behavior, I was unable to hold on to them. I found myself divorced with a pocket full of money because of an excellent job I had landed with Honeywell. It was a perfect recipe for disaster. Having a full time job helped to keep me somewhat out of trouble, but the good Lord knows I still tried to mess up my life.

At Honeywell, I repaired electronic circuit boards. Once again, I found myself the only black among a sea of white faces. I did well and, at one point, survived a layoff when the boss had to choose between me and an older, steady, white worker with a wife and kids. He chose me. I asked him if it was because of some kind of quota system by which he had to keep a black person, and he said no. He said, "You earned the position."

One day, while driving home from work, a state trooper patrol car was behind me. He followed me for a while then turned on his lights to pull me over. He saw a black man coming from the suburbs driving a Pontiac Riviera and just knew I was up to no good. I had two joints in the ashtray and was ready to light one up. He asked for my license and registration, which I gave him, and, in turn, I asked him why he pulled me over. He responded, "I saw something leaking out of your tail pipe."

Again, thank God for his mercy and grace because the cop just let me go.

I was a professional sinner, trying my best to get busted and possibly lose my great job. Nobody had to teach me to sin; it just came naturally.

I was on my motorcycle one day, heading home after playing chess at a friend's house. I had a pound of marijuana tucked inside my jacket when two officers told me to pull over. They were riding behind me and, for a split second, I considered trying to evade them. Then I thought, *no way they could know I had that pound of marijuana with me*, so I just pulled over. They said I was driving without a license plate. "I started out with one this morning when I left the house," I said. One of them took a closer look and could see a piece of the plate still under the screws, so he believed me. It's a good thing they didn't have the drug-sniffing dogs around.

Again, God's Grace allowed me to walk away from that situation.

* * *

I moved out of Cambridge, Massachusetts to New Hampshire to try to escape the drugs. My spirit was telling me I needed a change. A few years after living in New Hampshire, I moved to St. Thomas, still chasing a dream. My ex-wife and kids had moved there and I had visions of reconciling with my family. That didn't work because I really hadn't changed. I changed location, but not my person. I was still getting high, drunk and playing the fool. I was very fortunate to land another great job about a year after I got there. I started working with IBM, but the big difference was that I was just another black among all the employees.

Around that time in my life, four things happened that helped to shape my future. First, I had a close brush with death when I went back to Cambridge on vacation several years after moving to St. Thomas.

I was walking from Central Square to Harvard square with an old girlfriend, talking about the good old times. I was high, as usual, and dressed to kill. *How prophetic this last sentence almost turned out.*

Suddenly, a white man came up behind us and said, **"Excuse me,"** and then he pushed us as he walked by.

"The next time you say excuse me, give us a chance to move."

He stopped and turned around facing us, with his hands on his hips and said, **"The next time, I'll just stomp on you."**

Now, I was thinking he was a real fresh, young, white boy that needed to be taught a lesson. As the distance between us shrank, I was planning to hit him in the mouth. Sarah said, **"Just let him go."** This statement hooked my Adult.

Sarah was my guardian angel that night. She saved my life. I listened and when I got up close to the man, I said, **"You said excuse me, so let's leave it at that."**

At that moment, he showed me a large knife he was holding and said, **"This is your lucky day."** I then realize the magnitude of the situation. That person was out to kill someone that night. I was the perfect candidate. I was high and dressed like a pimp and he almost baited me into throwing the first punch.

I thank the Lord for sending an Angel to protect me.

The second thing that shaped my life, was accepting Jesus Christ as my personal Lord and Savior. There wasn't much of a change outwardly, but God started doing things on the inside.

The third was reading the book, *What Do You Say after You Say Hello?* After reading the book, I started what evolved into a long walk about how to communicate.

The fourth was meeting and marrying my wife who has been a solid rock in my life. She has taught me how to love and to give love.

* * *

My first daughter was born when I was only nineteen years old. I didn't know anything about fatherhood, but I had plenty of opportunity to learn. I met my second daughter on my return home after the service. It was a love rivaled only by what I felt for my first daughter.

After my ex-wife left St. Thomas, I was a single parent every summer when my two children came to stay with me. We had some memorable times during those summers. I remember trying to convince them to start their own business by shining shoes, in town, for money. I began by showing them how to shine shoes and then I let them practice on me. The next day, I wore a pair of shoes to work that they had shined and I fell to the ground about three times. I kept slipping and sliding everywhere I went. When I got home I told them about my weird day at work and about how I was unable to stand up. Then my oldest daughter said, **"Maybe it's because I polished the bottom of your shoes."**

"Why did you do that?" I exclaimed.

"Dad, you told me to polish your shoes, you didn't specify which parts."

At least I knew why I was falling all over the place. We had a good laugh over that.

Another time, I asked them to fix me dinner from leftovers from the previous night. I started on the pigs' feet, sucking the hell out of them trying to find some meat or juice. I couldn't find any. Instead of giving me leftovers, they had given me the used bones from the day before that we were saving for the dogs.

We truly had some great times together.

* * *

I was always the marrying type and found myself engaged about four or five times during my early thirties. I was in my thirties and still hell bent on my own destruction. Once, while driving home drunk, I fell asleep. The Holy Spirit woke me up as the car was about to plunge off the cliff.

Gladys also saved my life. She is now my wife of the last thirty-eight years and will always be, if I have my way. I don't remember the circumstances of when we first met, but the second time I saw her must have been about two years later. I asked her cousin to introduce us. She said she didn't want to meet me again. I asked, "Again? When was the first time?"

She must have been a little girl that first time around because I had never seen this woman before in my life. I was infatuated with her. More than love at first sight, I wondered where has she been all my life.

Before I could go out with her, I had to go to Puerto Rico to meet her parents—nice traditional family. When her father and I sat down, the first thing he did was to take his gun off his ankle and place it on the table. I asked, **"What is the gun for?"**

He said, **"Oh, don't pay that any mind; I just took it off to relax."**

Talk about a big, white elephant being in the room.

We were married six months later and this August will be thirty-eight years of blissful marriage.

From almost the very beginning I communicated to her about the Parent, Adult, and Child. I told her if we used this tool between us we will be giving our marriage its best chance to endure.

We have had our ups and downs and tragedies like most families but we managed to survive. The biggest tragedy was of my own making. Sayette, our first child, was born on Christmas day and when the doctor told me she was a girl, I told God to take her back. I wanted a boy.

Well, God did take her back two months later. The medical reason she died was of an enlarged heart. But I know the real reason is those awful words I spoke over her. Our words are so powerful, and because of ignorance, we utter stupid things all the time.

The Bible says, *"Life and death is in the power of the tongue, I place before you both, so choose life." (Deuteronomy. 30:19)*

Even when Sayette was in the emergency room surrounded by doctors, God spoke to me and said, **"Go in between all those doctors and lay your hands on her, and she will recover."** I was too scared to obey. What if it didn't work? I wished I had that same unquestioning God-kind-of faith that I had when I was young.

At the funeral for Sayette, a coworker spoke prophecy into my life. He said, "The next baby you have will be a boy and then you will get the girl back." It came to pass exactly as he had said.

I stepped up my sinful lifestyle by including cocaine into the mix. I reached an all-time low when the drug dealer told me one day, because of my drug use, he was going to own my house. Spiraling out of control, I didn't know what to do with myself. When I was sober, I wanted to be high. Ironically, when I was high I wanted to be sober. Thinking about what the drug dealer had told me brought me to a crossroad. I had a simple choice to make: choose life which was my family, home, job, and self-respect or continue down the path of destruction and lose everything. I was so bad that I snorted coke around my son when I thought he wasn't looking. He was about four at the time.

"Daddy," he said, "Why do you keep making that sound, sniff, sniff?"

That is when I knew it was time to come clean.

The next day, I told my wife what was going on and I called my boss and told him I needed help with my addiction. My boss did help by sending me to a drug clinic for two weeks and I was able to kick my habit.

My wife replied in her Adult and stayed calm and collected during my admission. I knew then I was going to make it.

Again Grace and Mercy showed up just in the nick of time.

The final hurdle came when my wife said she couldn't stand the smell of alcohol on my breath every night. She said I had to stop drinking or she would sleep somewhere else [Parent]. So, I stopped drinking and that was over thirty years ago [Adult]. She literally saved my life by giving me that ultimatum.

With drugs and alcohol out of the picture, I started a long walk with God and family. Because of my son, I started going to church on a regular basis. He was and is such a joy to me. When he was about five or six years old and something frightened him, like the barking of a dog, he would throw up both his arms, indicating that he wanted me to pick him up and protect him. When he played little league baseball, it gave me a thrill just watching him play. In one particular game, someone hit a fly ball to him and as he was zeroing in on it, I was so nervous. At the last second, he caught the ball, not with his glove, but with his hand. I cheered so loud and long because I was so proud of him. Now my son is six feet six and has a great job as a welder for the local government.

I am proud of all my children. The two oldest have their own families and have given me wonderful grandchildren and a great grand-child.

My youngest daughter has finished law school. When I told her about this book and that it only had eighty six pages, she said, "Now that sounds like a book I might actually read."

She understands the concepts and how it works and how to use them as well as anyone I've explained them to. If I raise my voice over an issue, she says, **"Is that your Child?"** I have to laugh, because she is right.

IT'S ALL ABOUT JESUS AND HIS WORD

As a young boy, I had a recurring thought when I got ready to go to sleep. It was not a nightmare because I would be awake trying to fall asleep when the thought came, but it was extremely scary to me. The thought was living forever in heaven and never dying. This freaked me out. You could live a thousand years in heaven, then ten thousand years, then a million years, and on and on, forever and ever. The concept of forever just scared me. When I came across scriptures that said, *"For my thoughts are not your thoughts, neither are your ways my ways, saith the Lord. For as the heavens are higher than the earth, so are my ways higher than your ways, and my thoughts than your thoughts"* (Isaiah 54: 8-9). That put everything into perspective for me. So, I stopped trying to figure Him out. That gave my sanity a break; I decided to trust that God had it all under control. That is a classic example of the Adult taking charge over the Child because of new and updated information.

I am in a ministry that teaches the uncompromising Word of God. In the middle of a service, I heard God, through the pastor, telling me to write this book.

"God, I don't know how to write."

"Just start, and let's see where it goes."

He told me the tool would help people to communicate better.

"Why do you think I kept you around for so long? I had plenty of chances to let the enemy take you out, but I don't want this story to end that way. You just be obedient and I will take care of the rest."

So, here I am, adding my story to this book that God told me to write.

"I no longer follow after my sinful nature; I am being led by the Holy Spirit."

It's a wonderful life. I truly have come full circle. I am regaining the ruthless trust I had in God when I was young. I just believe He is and have no doubt as to His absolute, *"Word of His Power. (Hebrews. 1:3)*

The ministry I am in now is just the culmination of all the other ministries I have been affiliated with.

No gimmick. No hype. Just Jesus.

The Pastor empowered me to write this story. A story that God told me his people needed to hear.

It's a story of how to communicate and it's also a love affair that God has with me and you and all who believe in Him.

CONCLUSION

There's nothing wrong with having a strong Parent or Child. They do have their place. But it is imperative to develop a strong Adult at some point in your life.

A Parent is important for the military, schoolteachers, police officers and many other fields too numerous to mention. It has its place. Giving commands, instructions, options, directives, and so forth and so on are all part of the Parent.

The Child is also important. When someone tells a good joke, you are supposed to laugh. When you feel pain or hurt, it is okay to cry or show emotion. Like the Parent, the (Child) also has countless situations for expression.

The point of this book is to understand the tool as outlined and be able to navigate between the different ego states as appropriate. When I find that I can't communicate with someone, I don't get frustrated anymore. I can quickly reason why and I just move on.

Next time someone starts to go off on you, ask, "Is that your Child?"

Or, if they tell you to do this or that, tell them you don't want to see their Parent.

I'm looking for a few good Adults.

ACKNOWLEDGMENTS

A special thanks to Gladys, my ideal wife, who was the first person to read this manuscript and provide me with her valuable ideas. Gladys also is the person who helped make this book materialize!

Thank you, Tonia, my delightful daughter, who did the first editing and made this manuscript actually look like a book.

Thanks to Annette, another perfect daughter, who provided the title for this book.

Also, I would like to thank Frank and Jasmine for their feedback which were very encouraging to me. Frank also helped with the editing which was extremely invaluable.

Special thanks to Milli and Rudy. The suggestions you made brought clarity to this book.

Maureen Hunte and special thanks to you for editing.

Last, but not least, I would like to thank my Pastor, Jason Jordan, who inspired me to write.

ABOUT THE AUTHOR

Basic Electronic technology was taught in my high school and gave me the background for a lifetime work. After high school, I went into the Air Force and continued my study in electronics.

After the Air Force, I worked for major electronic companies for the past forty-four years which include: Honeywell, IBM, Kodak, and Toshiba.

Watching my father read, when I was a young boy, implanted in me the curiosity to know what was in books. He instilled in me the love of reading. Thus, my journey began. I started selecting books at random based on what was on their covers. Most of the time, the books had nothing to do with their titles, but once I started reading a book, I wouldn't put it down for fear of missing something important.

My formal education comes from reading. I have read books on every subject under the sun.

Everything we need to know comes from books. I built a three level deck, forty feet by thirty feet, for my house just by reading the book called "Decks 1-2-3"

Whenever I saw a library on a television show, I knew that one day, my house would also have a library.

My love for reading has evolved to where I want to share some of the highlights with other people. This is the seed from which this book was birthed.

I live in the Virgin Islands. My wife and I have been married for thirty-eight years and we have two beautiful children and one grandchild. I also have two children and three grandchildren and a great-grandchild from a previous marriage.

ABOUT THE BOOK

Have you ever been in a conversation that went sideways on you and you didn't know why. Sure you have, we all have, and it doesn't matter whether it was with your spouse, children, friends, client, boss or employee. You found yourself at a loss because you didn't know what caused the sudden shift in direction.

That is what this book is about. "Adult conversations" will give you the tools to redirect the conversation where it belongs or signal you that it is time to shut it down.

My hope is that through my stories, this tool or concept can be passed on and applied in your daily life. Nothing comes easily. Using this communication tool takes time and patience.

Robert.Sr1313@gmail.com